King Cobra/ Cobra real

By Audry Graham   **Tradución al español: Nathalie Beullens**

Gareth Stevens
Publishing

Please visit our Web site, www.garethstevens.com. For a free color catalog of all our high-quality books, call toll free 1-800-542-2595 or fax 1-877-542-2596.

Cataloging Data

Graham, Audry.
King cobra / Cobra real
    p. cm. — (Killer snakes / Serpientes asesinas)
ISBN 978-1-4339-4557-1 (library binding
1. King cobra—Juvenile literature. I. Title.
QL666.O64G73 2011
597.96'42—dc22

                                    2010030696

First Edition

Published in 2011 by
Gareth Stevens Publishing
111 East 14th Street, Suite 349
New York, NY 10003

Copyright © 2011 Gareth Stevens Publishing

Designer: Michael J. Flynn
Editor: Greg Roza
Spanish translation: Nathalie Beullens

Photo credits: Cover, pp. 1, (2–4, 6, 8, 10, 12, 14, 16, 18, 20–24 snake skin texture), 5, 7, 11, 15 (main image), 21 Shutterstock.com; p. 9 Joe McDonald/Visuals Unlimited/Getty Images; p. 13 iStockphoto.com; pp. 15 (fangs and venom), 19 Mattias Klum/National Geographic/Getty Images; p. 17 ZSSD/Minden Pictures/Getty Images.

Printed in the United States of America

CPSIA compliance information: Batch #CW11GS: For further information contact Gareth Stevens, New York, New York at 1-800-542-2595.

Contents

Contenido

Boldface words appear in the glossary/
Las palabras en **negrita** aparecen en el glosario

King of the Cobras

The king cobra is the longest **venomous** snake in the world! They can grow up to 18 feet (5.5 m) long and weigh up to 20 pounds (9 kg). Their venom is deadly. One king cobra bite has enough venom to kill an elephant!

- -

La reina de las cobras

¡La cobra real es la serpiente **venenosa** más larga del mundo! Puede crecer hasta 18 pies (5.5 m) de largo y pesar hasta 20 libras (9 kg). Su veneno es mortal. ¡La mordida de una cobra real tiene suficiente veneno para matar a un elefante!

5

King Cobras at Home

King cobras are found in Southeast Asia and parts of India. They live in wooded places and open plains. King cobras can be light brown, dark brown, or greenish-brown. They may have white, brown, or yellow stripes. Their bellies are yellow or white.

La cobra real en casa

Las cobras reales se encuentran en el sureste de Asia y partes de India. Viven en lugares boscosos y llanuras abiertas. Las cobras reales pueden ser marrón claro, marrón oscuro o marrón verdoso. Pueden tener rayas blancas, marrones o amarillas. Sus vientres son amarillos o blancos.

Asia/Asia

KEY/CLAVE
king cobra/
cobra real

In the Nest

Female king cobras lay between 20 and 50 eggs at one time. They are the only snakes that make nests for their eggs. The adult king cobra keeps the eggs safe until the babies **hatch** about 60 to 90 days later. Each baby is about 20 inches (51 cm) long.

En el nido

Las cobras reales hembras ponen entre 20 y 50 huevos en una sola vez. Son las únicas serpientes que hacen un nido para sus huevos. La cobra real adulta cuida los huevos hasta que los bebés **salen del cascarón**, entre 60 y 90 días más tarde. Cada bebé mide unas 20 pulgadas (51 cm) de largo.

9

Stay Away!

The king cobra is easily angered. It **attacks** quickly when it is surprised. Sudden movements make it strike, too. When a king cobra is scared or angry, it flattens its neck and spreads it out to make itself look bigger. This is called a hood.

¡Aléjate!

La cobra real se enoja fácilmente. La cobra real **ataca** muy rápida cuando está sorprendida. También ataca cuando ve movimientos repentinos. Cuando una cobra real está enojada o asustada aplana su cuello para parecer más grande de lo que es. A esto se le llama una capucha.

hood/capucha

The king cobra has short **fangs**. To make up for this, it raises its head up to 5 feet (1.5 m) off the ground. Then it brings its head down quickly and drives its fangs into its enemy. It can also strike from 7 feet (2.1 m) away!

La cobra real tiene **colmillos** cortos. Para compensar, levanta su cabeza hasta 5 pies (1.5 m) del piso, después baja la cabeza rápidamente y clava los colmillos en su enemigo. ¡Además, puede atacar desde una distancia de 7 pies (2.1 m)!

13

King Cobra Venom

King cobra venom isn't very strong compared to other snake venom. However, a king cobra bite has much more venom in it than the bites of other venomous snakes. This makes it one of the deadliest snakes in the world.

El veneno de la cobra real

El veneno de la cobra real no es tan fuerte como el de otras serpientes. Sin embargo, una mordida de la cobra real tiene más veneno que la mordida de otras serpientes venenosas. Por eso, es una de las serpientes más mortales del mundo.

**fangs and venom/
colmillos y veneno**

On the Hunt

The king cobra hunts mainly during the day. It eats mostly other snakes. Some also eat lizards, eggs, and small **mammals**. King cobras don't spread their hoods or rise up when attacking **prey**. These actions are just a warning for their enemies.

A cazar se ha dicho

Generalmente, la cobra real caza durante el día y come, principalmente, otras serpientes. Algunas cobras comen lagartijas, huevos y pequeños **mamíferos**. Las cobras reales no despliegan sus capuchas cuando atacan una **presa**. Sólo lo hacen cuando quieren prevenir a sus enemigos.

17

A king cobra uses its tongue to smell its prey. It also has excellent eyesight. It can see prey 300 feet (91 m) away. The king cobra attacks quickly. Its venom **stuns** or kills the prey. Then the king cobra eats the prey whole.

La cobra real usa su lengua para oler su presa. También tiene una vista excelente, puede ver a su presa a 300 pies (91 m) de distancia. La cobra real ataca rápidamente. Su veneno **aturde** a su víctima, a la que después se come entera.

19

People and King Cobras

King cobras don't like to be around people. This is good for people! Very few people die from king cobra bites each year. However, king cobras attack people when they're scared, surprised, or have no way to escape. One bite can kill a person in just 15 minutes!

La gente y las cobras reales

A las cobras reales no les gusta estar cerca de la gente. ¡Menos mal! Muy poca gente muere a causa de mordidas de cobras reales cada año. Sin embargo las cobra reales atacan a la gente cuando tienen miedo, están sorprendidas o no se pueden escapar. ¡Una mordida puede matar a una persona en 15 minutos!

Snake Facts/Hoja informativa

King Cobra/Cobra real

Length/ Longitud	up to 18 feet (5.5 m) long hasta 18 pies (5.5 m) de largo
Weight/Peso	up to 20 pounds (9 kg) hasta 20 libras (9 kg)
Where It Lives/ Hábitat	Southeast Asia and parts of India sureste de Asia y partes de India
Life Span/ Años de vida	about 20 years unos 20 años
Killer Fact/ Datos mortales	King cobras sway from side to side as their enemy moves. This is one reason why **snake charmers** use them in their acts. Most king cobra bites happen to snake charmers! Las cobras reales se mecen de lado a lado siguiendo el movimiento de su enemigo ¡Es por eso que los **encantadores de serpiente** las usan en sus espectáculos! La mayor parte de las mordidas de cobra son a los encantadores.

Glossary/Glosario

attack: to try to harm someone or something

fang: a sharp tooth

hatch: to break out of an egg

mammal: an animal that has live young and feeds them milk from the mother's body

prey: an animal hunted by other animals for food

snake charmer: someone who handles snakes and dances to music with them

stun: to shock something so it can't move

venomous: able to produce a liquid called venom that is harmful to other animals

- -

atacar tratar de dañar a alguien o a algo

aturdir causar un choque a algo para que otro no se pueda mover

colmillo (el) diente afilado

encantador de serpiente (el) alguien que adiestra serpientes y baila con ellas

mamífero (el) un animal que tiene bebés y los alimenta con leche que proviene de su cuerpo

presa (la) un animal cazado por otro animal para comérselo

salir del cascarón cuando nacen los animales de un huevo

venenoso(a) capaz de producir veneno que es dañino para otros animales

For More Information/Más información

Books/Libros

Mattern, Joanne. *King Cobras.* Mankato, MN: Capstone Press, 2010.

White, Nancy. *King Cobras: The Biggest Venomous Snakes of All!* New York, NY: Bearport Publishing, 2009.

Web Sites/Páginas en Internet

King Cobra

animals.nationalgeographic.com/animals/reptiles/king-cobra/
Read more about the king cobra.

King Cobras Lock Horns

animal.discovery.com/videos/king-cobra-and-i-cobras-lock-horns.html
Watch a video of two king cobras fighting. Also includes links to other king cobra videos.

Publisher's note to educators and parents: Our editors have carefully reviewed these Web sites to ensure that they are suitable for students. Many Web sites change frequently, however, and we cannot guarantee that a site's future contents will continue to meet our high standards of quality and educational value. Be advised that students should be closely supervised whenever they access the Internet.

Nota de la editorial a los padres y educadores: Nuestros editores han revisado con cuidado las páginas en Internet para asegurarse de que son apropiadas para niños. Sin embargo, muchas páginas en Internet cambian con frecuencia, y no podemos garantizar que sus contenidos futuros sigan conservando nuestros elevados estándares de calidad y de interés educativo. Tengan en cuenta que los niños deben ser supervisados atentamente siempre que accedan a Internet.

Index/Índice